LEABHARLANNA CHONTAE FHINE GALL
FINGAL COUNTY LIBRARIES
GARRISTOWN LIBRARY
PH: 8355020

Items should be returned on or before the last date shown below. Items may be renewed by personal application, writing, telephone or by accessing the online Catalogue Service on Fingal Libraries' website. To renew give date due, borrower ticket number and PIN number if using online catalogue. Fines are charged on overdue items and will include postage incurred in recovery. Damage to, or loss of items will be charged to the borrower

Date Due	Date Due	Date Due
05. 03. 18,		

SHIPS IN EARLY IRISH HISTORY

BY
MEIKE BLACKWELL

BALLINAKELLA PRESS,
Whilegate, Co. Clare, Ireland.

© 1992.
Designs and setting Ballinakella Press.
Text Meike Blackwell.

First published by Ballinakella Press,
Whitegate, County Clare, in 1992.
All rights Reserved.

[BL] British Library Cataloguing in Publication Data.
A catalogue record for this book is available
from the British Library.

ISBN 0 946538 21 2

Author: Meike Blackwell.
Editor: Hugh W. L. Weir.
Word Processing: Grania R. Weir.
Design: Tomás J. Porcell.
Cover Design: Hugh W. L. Weir + Tomás J. Porcell.

I dedicate this book to my husband Joe.

With grateful acknowledgement of the generosity of

IARNRÓD ÉIREANN - IRISH RAIL

towards the cost of producing this book.

CONTENTS.

LIST OF ILLUSTRATIONS.

ACKNOWLEDGEMENTS.

My special thanks to Joe and my children Alex, Kirstin and Peter for all their help and to Dr. Gerald Lyons, Dr. Roderick Peters, Mr. David Philips and Professor Christine Heym for correcting my often faulty English. Thanks also to the National Museum of Ireland; the Reading Museum and Art Gallery and The Corporation of Winchelsea, England; Antikvarisk-topografiska arkivet, Stockholm, Sweden; Universitetets Oldsaksamling (University Museum of National Antiquities), Oslo, Norway; Universitäts bibliothek, Heidelberg, Germany; the Viking Ship Restoration Committee, Evanston, U.S.A.; La Ville de Bayeux, France; Craggaunowen - The Living Past, a division of the Hunt Museums Trust, Ireland; The Manx Museum and National Trust, the Isle of Man; and to the Bodleian Library, Oxford, England for the use of (Laud Mis. 720, folio 226v) the XIII Century Giraldus Cambrensis drawing of two men in a boat on the front cover. I express appreciation to Grania and Hugh Weir and Tomás of Ballinakella Press for typesetting, editing and design of "Ships in Early Irish History".

Meike Blackwell
Newport, Co. Mayo.

INTRODUCTION

MAN'S FIRST ARRIVAL, CA. 680 BC.

Ireland, on the westernmost edge of Europe is an island and as such can only be reached by crossing the surrounding waters. Boats, rafts and ships have played a key role in her history ever since the ice started retreating from its shores.

Sometime between 9000 B.C. and 7000 B.C. the ice, which was then covering Ireland up to a depth of about seven hundred meters, started to melt and retreat northwards. As a consequence the landmass slowly rose as the weight of the ice lessened. But far up in the North, vast amounts of water remained locked up in the ice keeping the waterlevel between Ireland and the West coast of England very much lower than it is today. Some sources say it was as much as twenty-five meters lower at that time. As there are only a scant thirteen miles of water between North Eastern Ireland and the western edge of Scotland today, it follows that in around 7-6000 B.C. the distance between these countries was even less.

The first reliably dated human remains ever found in Ireland bring us back to approximately 6800 B.C. They were discovered in the North East corner, in county Antrim. Thus man's first appearance in Ireland may well have been by way of this stretch of water, and he must have come in some kind of vessel.

To date no one has found the remains of any kind of boat, raft or canoe of this period anywhere near this area of the East coast of Ireland. However through associated finds, such as fish bones, shell heaps and stone tools, we know definietly that man came over to Ireland at this time and that he remained.

By about 3700 B.C., the Neolithic people arrived following the same sea route and pushed the original family groups further south and west. But once again there are as yet no visible remains of boats, although a simple raft boat, a dugout canoe or a skin covered boat were by then within the means of the people to build.

VI

As wood is easily destroyed by bacteria and fungi, wind and weather, and even man himself, the chances of survival over such a long expanse of time are very limited. Only a boat that had silted over or sunk in a bog would survive and may one day be found. Meanwhile we must depend on written records about the early Irish and their boats.

The Hedin Stone showing Ogham and Runic inscriptions and Early Ship, Kirk Maughold, *(Manx National Heritage)*.

CHAPTER 1

FIRST MENTION OF IRELAND AND IRISH BOATS.

The oldest surviving records of Ireland, its inhabitants and their use of boats date from the fourth ce ntury B.C.

The story of Himilco the Phoenician comes to us via the 'Ora Maritima' a geographical textbook compiled by the Roman Rufus Festus Avienus around 425 B.C. Avienus is said to have seen these records in a temple in Carthage in the fourth century and subsequently wrote the story in verse. Only one, much later, version of the Ora Maritima survives, the one compiled by Pisanus of Venice in 1488 A.D.

In this manuscript Himilco is said to have sailed northwards along the coast of Spain between Gades, the modern Cadiz, and Galicia and across the ocean to the Insula Albionum (Scotland?) - Scottish Isles?, England and on to Hibernia, Ireland, which he found heavily populated. He mentioned that the Irish people were active traders and "undertook their many journeys by sea in boats sewn together from skins". According to him, they had no knowledge of how to build wooden boats.

In these early centuries the Phoenicians were actively sailing the seas and collecting tin not only from Spain and Cornwall, but also from the Oestrimunidas, or Tin Isles, now known as the Scilly Islands. To them it was a well known fact, that Ireland, the 'Sacred Island', inhabited by the Hibernii, lay at a distance of only two days further sailing. However, to date only a single tin ingot, of the kind also known from Cyprus, has been so far found. It came to light in Falmouth harbour in Cornwall and provides the only visible proof of trade with the Phoenicians.

According to Thomas Moore there had been a Greek poem 'Argonautics' from approximately 500 B.C., telling of a vague dream of the Atlantic, in which Ireland alone, under the Celtic name of 'Iernis', is glanced at, without any reference whatever to Britain.

Moore then went on; "It is thought, moreover, to have been by special information, direct from the Phoenicians, that the poet acquired this knowledge..."

Gaius Julius Caesar is our next source of indirect information about possible types of Irish boats. "Their ships were built and rigged in a different manner from ours," he wrote in 50 B.C. after having encountered the Celts in Northwest Gaul. He goes on to say that the keel and ribs were made of light timber and the hull wrought in wickerwork and covered with hides.

Ptolemy, a second century A.D. Egyptian astronomer and geographer who lived in Alexandria, had on his maps more details and correct locations of promontories and rivers for Ireland than for England. As he too had gained his knowledge from the Phoenicians, it seems to prove that, in those days at least, Ireland was better known than Britain. His maps remained the only authoritiative works till the fifteenth century.

Comparison of Ptolemy's map with one of modern Ireland

Tacitus, the Roman historian, who lived at the end of the first century A.D., also wrote in his 'Histories', that the waters and harbours of Ireland were better known, through commerce and navigators, than those of Britain.

In 300 A.D. Caius Julius Solinus wrote the book 'Collectanea Rerum Memorabilium or Polihistor'. In book No. XXIII entitled 'Brittannia' he stated "Mare quod Hiberniam et Britanniam interluit, undosum inquietumque toto in anno, nonnisi pauculis diebus est navigabile. Navigant autem vimineis alevis, quos circumdant ambitione tergorum bubulorum: quantocumque tempore cursus tenebit, navigantes escis abstinent." which translates; "The sea which separates Hibernia from Britain, is rough and stormy throughout the year: it is navigable for a few days only; they voyage in small boats formed of pliant twigs, covered with skins of oxen. During the time they are at sea the voyagers abstain from food."

Pliny, who lived and wrote at the end of the first and beginning of the second century A.D., had more specific information when he wrote his 'Naturalis Historia' somewhere between 70 and 80 A.D. "Ireland lies beyond Britain" he said, "the shortest crossing being from the district of the Silures, (South Wales), a distance of 30 miles!" He went on to say that the Roman Agrippa believed the island to be 600 (1) miles long and 300 miles wide. He also credited the historian Timaeus with the observation that the.... "Britons cross in boats of osier covered with stitched hides..."

Cormac MacArt, the Irish king, compiled a book of Rights in the third century. In it he mentions an annual tribute of ten ships with beds being paid by the king of Cashel to the High King, or Ard Rí. The book of Acaill, possibly also compiled by Cormac, contains the Muir Brethra - the Sea Laws - which define the rights and duties of foreign trading vessels, without however mentioning what kind of ships they were. The fact that there was a need for a Sea Law indicates that there were sea going vessels. Again in Cormac's Glossary one can read that Brecan, the grandson of Niall of the Nine Hostages, had a trading fleet of fifty curraghs sailing between Ireland and Scotland. Unfortunately these were swallowed up by the whirlpool off Rathlin Island, which even today is still called 'Coire Breccain', (Brecan's Whirlpool). Niall himself is said to have raided

3

Wales in a fleet of curraghs at the end of the fourth century, a fleet apparently so great it prompted the poet Claudian to write "..the ocean foamed with hostile oars."

The ancient Irish laws, the Brehon Laws, which had evolved very slowly over the centuries, had finally been written down at the request of St. Patrick sometime in the fifth century. P.W. Joyce has written, "In the year 438 A.D. a collection of the Pagan laws was made at the request of St. Patrick, and the whole Fenechas Code (the law of the free land tillers) was expounded to him by Dubthach, the king's chief poet, a zealous Christian convert.." In one of these Brehon Laws there is a fixed list of payments due a master ship builder, also called an ollave builder, for specific tasks. Constructing any of the following boats brought him four cows each. They were:

1. lung -- navis longa (large sea going vessels)
2. barc -- scapha
   (smaller boats for coastal trade like dugouts or rafts).
3. curach -- caruca (skin boats)

Wooden-built boats do seem to have been known to the Irish, even if they probably did not build them themselves.

However, the only surviving visible evidence of early Irish boats are two small representations, one in gold and one carved on stone, which will be discussed later, and some dugout canoes found in bogs. The latter are difficult to date and probably span a long period of time.

NOTE. (1) 1 mile = 1. 609 Kms.

CHAPTER 2

DUGOUTS-
LOGBOATS.

Dugouts, also variously called logboats or canoes, may well have been the means by which the first settlers arrived in Ireland some 8000 years ago. At that time, during the Mesolithic (middle stone age) period man had already acquired the knowledge of how to use the axe, wedge and hammer, and hollowing out a log lay well within his means.

To date some one hundred and fifty prehistoric logboats have been found in Ireland and Scotland as well as over one hundred and

Single-piece Canoe from Cahore, Co. Wexford.

seventy in England. In 1991 two log boats were definately dated by radiocarbon to the Neolithic period of approximately 2550-2450 yet none have so far been either found or dated near the earliest settled site in Ireland. Large deposits, however, of fish bones from deep sea fish along the Scottish West coast as well as

Single-piece Canoe from the Boyne.

axe blades made from the flint found in Ulster quarries have been found and dated, proving that at least longer sea voyages were possible and, indeed, undertaken.

Dugouts, as the name implies, wer cut out of single tree such as

Single-piece Canoe from Toome Bar *(Wood-Martin)*.

pines or oaks using fire and tools such as axes and adzes. This process was of necessity a long drawn out task; quite frequently it was not completed within one season or even a year or two. This was especially true if the chosen tree was still green and had to be prevented from drying out and splitting. In such cases the unfinished canoe was stored under water until the work could recommence. Posts were driven into the bottom of the lake or sea; the boat was loaded with stones and sunk between them, where it remained till it was ready to be finished.

The efficiency of a large logboat could be improved through extension and expansion of its sides by softening them with water and fire and then forcing them apart with wooden struts. Also, by lifting up the ends of the canoe so that they were higher than the sides, the onrushing waters could be deflectd sideways rather than come crashing in over the bow. At other times a single plank was also added and sewn to each side, thus raising each and making the dugout more sea worthy. Another means of enlarging a canoe was to cut the logboat in half lengthwise and add some planks between the halves and so widen the boat considerably. It is not without reason that the dugout is often referred to as the "grandfather" of most boat types.

The early dugouts found in Irish waters come mostly from the viscinity of crannogs in lakes or near river banks. A crannog is an ancient man-made island which was inhabited by the early Irish for defensive purposes. However this does not rule out dugouts having been used as sea going vessels. Roughly speaking, the known Irish canoe may be classified into three types. Acording to Wood-Martin they are:

1. A canoe averaging about seven metres in length and eighty centimetres in width and having either pointed or rounded ends with a round or flat bottom.

2. One much larger, up to thirteen metres long and round at the bow but square at the stern. The latter is made from a separate piece of wood and so added to the overall weight of the canoe.

3.   This is trough shaped, small at only 3 - 4 metres in length and square at both ends with a rounded bottom. It is equipped with handles at either end for carrying.

Another early author, Sir James Ware, in 1654 wrote in his book 'The Antiquities and History of Ireland' that the Irish called the dugout the "Gotti" and the hide covered boats "Gorraghs" from which the later word "curach" and then the anglicized version "curragh" were derived.

CHAPTER 3

SKIN COVERED BOATS, CURRAGHS AND CORACLES.

"A portable vessel of wicker ordinarily used by the wild Irish", runs a description of these boats in the seventeenth century.

It is quite possible that even in the earliest times, the skin covered boat was a more sea worthy craft for the rough waters around Ireland and Britain than any other vessel, be it a raft or a hollowed out log.

Even today curraghs are still built in the time honoured tradition of first laying down the gunwale, usually made of oak. Thus a curragh, and nowadays only a curragh, is built upside down. When the gunwale has the

An Upturned Curragh being transported.

shape and size required, first the ribs and then the stringers, which have been cut from pliable ash trees, are added and fastened. Today these are nailed on, but in prehistoric times and well into the middle ages they were secured with leather thongs. When the size of a curragh exceeds a certain length it requires additional support, which is provided by the insertion of thwarts. (1) A modern curragh is covered with canvas saturated with boiled tar or pitch to make it waterproof. In the early

A water-borne Curragh.

days however, oxhides were used, thus the name, 'skin covered boat'. These oxhides were sewn together and then waterproofed by soaking them in boiled mutton grease before stitching them onto the finished frame. Others used horsehides instead, as did the inhabitants of the Erris peninsula in Co. Mayo and those on Rathlin Island where one can read in an account book for the year 1760, "... paid for one mare's hide for the boat, 1s. and 6d...."

The earliest record of a skin boat having a cover other than hides is in 'The Irish Tourist, or the People and Provinces of Ireland,' a tourist guide, we would call it today, of 1837. It refers to the use of calico or flannel as covering for curraghs. Yet some years later, in 1853, C.H. Hartshorne reported that the curraghs of the Aran Islands were still covered with hides.

Curraghs are usually provided with long and narrow oars which pivot on thole pins so that feathering while rowing is impossible. Large curraghs, as in Co. Kerry, may still carry a lug sail attached to a mast of ash wood. Whereas nowadays the sail is made of cloth, it was woven from flax in the early days. A very similar method of construction was used for the Irish coracle as described by Wakeman in 1848 in the 'Journal of the Royal Historical and Archaeological Association of Ireland'

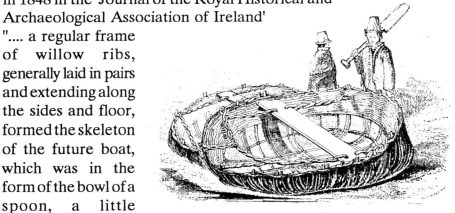

".... a regular frame of willow ribs, generally laid in pairs and extending along the sides and floor, formed the skeleton of the future boat, which was in the form of the bowl of a spoon, a little broader towards one end than the other;

Curragh, as used on the Boyne, 1848 *(Wakeman)*.

about 8' in length, but very nearly circular. The extremities of the ribs for a depth of about 18" from what would now be called the gunwale, were set in a very thick, strong and closely woven band of wicker-

9

work, above which the ends of the rods slightly projected. Midships was a thwart of ash or oak pierced with 4 holes, 2 near either end, through which were rove throngs, composed of twisted osiers connecting the seat, or thward, with various position of the above mentioned band, so as to bind the work together. The frame was then covered over on the outside with skin, untanned, of the horse or cow".

Today Irish curraghs survive only on the rugged and wild West coast. But even so, they still have distinguishing features according to their location. Thus, a typical curragh from Co. Donegal is rarely more than 3 meters to 4 meters in length and is often rather crudely fashioned. Further south in counties Mayo and Galway one finds curraghs of 5 meters to 6 meters and up to 7 meters to 8 meters long and built for two, three or four men. To the knowledgeable seaman, there are many local variations even among these. In Co. Kerry and particularly on the Dingle Peninsula one still finds the biggest and often most elegant curraghs, here called 'naomhog', or 'naevog'. They may be a good 8 meters or more long and are usually rigged for sailing. Almost all curraghs are 100-135 cm. wide regardless of region, and today may have square sterns to accommodate a small engine. As none have any kind of keel, they seem to skim across the water and when under sail, can only sail with the wind or at most on a broad reach. Being light in weight, they are often built at quite a distance from the water; when finished, three to four men simply crawl under them, lift them, and then march them down to the sea! The inland curragh or coracle, last seen on the Boyne river near Oldbridge in 1936, was smaller, a mere 2 meters by 1.5 meters.

It has been truly said that Irish curraghs, like the umiaks of the Eskimos, reached such a high state of development through sheer necessity due to the lack of suitable trees for plank-built boats.

NOTE. (1) See Glossary.

CHAPTER 4

BROIGHTER BOAT AND BANTRY BOAT

Two representations of prehistoric Irish boats deserve special mention. Both, the lovely little golden replica known as the 'Broighter Boat' and the relatively well preserved stone impression known as the 'Bantry Boat', are virtually all that remain to illustrate the pre Viking boats used in Ireland. True, a few dugout canoes of uncertain date have been found in bogs, but of the early sea-going vessels no physical trace has so far been discovered.

THE BROIGHTER BOAT

The Broighter Boat, now in the National Museum of Ireland, was found in 1895 by a ploughman in a field near Broighter in Co. Derry, together with a hoard of other gold objects. The boat had been badly damaged by the farmers plough and only after a goldsmith in Dublin brought it back into shape, was it recognizable as a boat. Its probable age was later determined by Hartmann (in 1970) through measuring the platinum content of the gold. This put it and the other gold objects into the La Tene period of the first century B.C.

The boat, rather roughly fashioned, was simply cut from a flat sheet of gold with slits at either end, which were then squeezed together until they overlapped very slightly. It has an overall length of 18.4 cm. a width of 7.6 cm. and a depth of 4.9 cm. The bow is slightly longer than the stern. Originally there must have been nine thwarts of which only eight were found. These are fastened to the hull of the boat by small rivets. The holes for the nine oars on either side are very slightly to the rear of the thwarts, indicating, perhaps, that the oarsmen sat with their back to the bow. The surviving fifteen oars are attached with thin gold wire to the holes. The mast is amidships and the steering oar, on the port side, is similarly fastened with gold wire. Further items belonging to the boat were a yard

The Broighter Boat, *(National Museum of Ireland)*.

pierced in the center to let the mast pass through, three forked poles and one fluked piece variously described as a grappling iron or anchor. The question whether this golden model is of a skin covered boat or of one built of planks has not yet been completely decided.

Whether it depicts a vessel of planks or of skin, the Broighter Boat remains the oldest surviving model of an Irish sea- going vessel.

THE BANTRY BOAT

The only other pre Viking boat representation is carved on a pillar stone near Bantry in Co. Cork. The stone still stands in an open field quite unprotected from wind, rain and sun and thus gets harder to study as the years go by. The pillar itself is some 3.5 meters tall and only 20.32 cm. across and has a very weathered appearance. On the East face of this stone is the carving of the vessel known as the Bantry Boat. It is hard to see with the naked eye and becomes clear only when viewed through the lens of a camera. It has an overall length of 50.8 cm. There are four oarsmen in the boat and one helmsman manning the steering oar. The boat also carries a small cross on its stern. All around it are carved crosses tempting some people to say that it is being rowed towards heaven over a sea of crosses. The bow of the boat is represented as rising forwards, much like a modern curragh still does in Co. Kerry. The whole boat seems to be high on the water or "skimming" over it and the oarsmen seem

The Bantry Boat.

13

to be pulling hard on their oars.   The helmsman is leaning well forward, holding the oar in his right hand, although it looks as if the steering oar itself is on the port side.   Even if one cannot be sure just how many men this vessel was meant to carry, it seems certain to be a skin covered boat and the carving has been dated as belonging to the eighth century A.D., well before any Viking plank boats are believed to have appeared in the Cork area.

The curious fact that both these boats seem to have their steering oar on the port side instead of the usual starboard is hard to explain.   In the Bantry Boat it could conceivably be an omission by the artist, but considering the quality and the realism of the rest of the carving this seems unlikely.   The Broighter Boat does have another hole on the starboard side of the stern; perhaps the steering oar was meant to be changed from side to side on demand, yet the golden thread for holding the oar in position was only on the port side.

CHAPTER 5

THE FOURTH TO SIXTH CENTURIES. IRISH EXPANSION

So far, except for the mention of the Brehon laws in Chapter One, we have been concerned mainly with logboats and skin covered boats in connection with Ireland. Yet it has long been believed that a Celtic way of shipbuilding existed. There is however, very little proof of this tradition outside of some poorly preserved coins and a few notes by ancient authors.

In 1937, a plank-built boat was discovered at Ferriby in Yorkshire, England. It was a flat boat, without keel, the broad planks lying side by side, sewn together with withys and then caulked with moss under the overlying laths. Its date was estimated as around 1500 B.C. Two further boat discoveries in the same estuary confirmed this in later years. A few years later another two ancient ships were found in England, one in 1958 at

The Oghan Stone, Maughold, Isle of Man *(Manx National Heritage)*.

Guys House in London and the other in 1962 at Blackfiars. Both have flat bottoms and no keel. The planks are of oak, as are the ribs, which were nailed on with thick iron nails, the points of which had then been bent. An interesting feature of these boats is the manner of caulking. Hazel twigs had been driven in between the planks without the use of pitch and tar. Ancient boats were usually built by adding the ribs after the actual body had been constructed; however, these two were built by the so called 'Skeleton method' whereby the ribs were formed first and the planks were added later. The remains of the boat from Blackfriars had signs of sea-worm tunnels, showing that the boat could have been in use at least along the English coast. Through associated finds, these two vessels have been dated as belonging to the second century A.D. which is well into the Roman period.

Ogham Stone, Silchester, Hants
(Reading Museum).

Considering the regular commerce between Ireland and England which must have gone on at that time, one can safely assume that the Irish at least knew of plank-built boats. Until we find one on Irish soil, we can only be certain of skin covered boats as Irish sea-going vessels.

In the late third and early fourth century A.D., Ireland's agriculture was expanding and the population was on the increase. It was then that the Irish Goidels, also called Scotti, started to raid and later settle on the Western coasts of Wales and Scotland. After 435 A.D. or thereabouts, when the Roman occupation of England came to an end, Irish invasions of these western shores were greatly facilitated and profitable. How far the Irish occupation and influence spread can be seen by looking at the distribution of Ogham stones in Britain. Ogham inscribed stones were the Irish equivalent of those with Scandinavian Runes. It was a way of inscribing or incising lines and notches, representing the letters of the Latin alphabet, on to the edge or arris or undressed standing stones. These were primarily memorial stones telling the names and often the background of some person or persons. Of the almost four hundred known Ogham stones remaining, there are some fifty four in Wales, Scotland, Devon and Cornwall, and one even as far East as Hampshire with a further six on the Isle of Man. Slowly Irish seaborn raids decreased and Irish settlers such as representaives of the tribes of Laigin and Deisi, who set up kingdoms in western Wales, stayed on British soil. However, unlike the Dal Riada from Northern Ireland who settled in western Scotland and remained there to become part of the land, they were not destined to survive for ever. The Isle of Man, settled by the Irish and named after the Irish god 'Manannan' was Irish for many centuries.

Was all this made possible by the use of plank-built boats, dugouts or skin boats? The fact is, that most northern European wooden boats developed from the dugout and that the skin covered boat remained quite unchanged; yet where the curragh met the dugout, it greatly influenced the improvement of the internal stiffening of plank-built boats.

Ireland not only benefitted materially by this early expansion across the sea, but was also brought into contact with Christianity which in turn spread out again from its shores with renewed vigor.

CHAPTER 6

EARLY IRISH SEAFARERS.

In the early Middle Ages Ireland was still so heavily wooded that travel was restricted to the inland waterways, the rivers and lakes, and the long, rugged and often stormy coastline.

On the inland waterways the raft, dugout canoe and its various other versions were satisfactory and reasonably safe, but on the open sea the curragh was dominant. By now this skin-covered boat had evolved sufficiently to be sea-worthy enough for use as the sole mode of long distance water transport.

A typical medieval skin boat had no keel, which prevented it from running against the wind or tacking. Its double gunwale was of oak and the ribs and stringers were of ash. Iron was still very scarce, so leather thongs were used to lash it together much like a present day wicker basket. This framework was then covered with oxhides which had first been stitched together and soaked in either raw wool grease or boiled mutton grease. The boat usually had two masts of ash which carried square sails woven from flax. Besides these, the boat was equipped with long oars and a steering paddle, both of which were also fashioned from ash.

During the sixth to the ninth centuries the Irish church enjoyed a period of great strength, prosperity and security. There were monasteries along most of the waterways, and the Irish monks and scholars were renowned for their learning. However, to an Irishman it was the ultimate sacrifice to leave his country and remain abroad. So the ascetic monks went out to spend their lives in dedicated and solitary prayer. This frequently evolved into missionary work and the founding of monasteries.

In fact, the religious inter-relationship between Ireland and England was so regular then, that one can read in Camden's 'Britannia'.... "Our Anglo-Saxons went at those times to Ireland as if to a fair to purchase goods. Hence it is frequently read in our historians of holy men, '(He was sent to Ireland to school' or 'He went to the Irish renowned for their Philosophy')" And they came not only from England but also from the European mainland.

An early Irish exile to leave Irish shores was *St. Columcille* who went in his skin-covered boat to Iona (1) in 563). He landed at Port a Churaich and is said to have destroyed his boat for fear his homesickness would tempt him to return to Ireland straight away. Although in the following years he crossed the sea many times, he was based on Iona until his death in 597.

Yet it was only after *St. Aidan* came to Lindisfarne, an island off the English East coast, in 634 and started his monastery there with the help of *St. Finnian* and *St. Colman,* that Christianity began to spread in earnest. St. Aidan had previously been with *St. Columcille* on Iona, but he originally hailed from Galway, a long boat journey from Lindisfarne. He too remained an exile and died at his monastery in 651.

St. Fursey went to East Anglia and North Eastern Gaul and *St. Finbar* of Connacht founded Glastonbury, while *St. Fridolin* started the monastery of Sackingen on the Rhine.

The urge to embrace a life in exile drove the monks further and further afield. *St. Gall,* a former disciple of St. Columbanus went to Switzerland and died there in 645. Later a monastery was founded there in his name and the modern town of *St. Gallen* still reminds us of this Irish monk.

St. Killian or Cilian, went to Wuerzburg in Germany where he was murdered in 689 and is still their patron saint. *St. Fergal* travelled to Salzburg where he remained until his death in 784.

One of the best remembered saints is *St. Columbanus* who lived from 539-615. Like the others, he set forth from his beloved Ireland in a skin boat probably with a few followers. He went first to France where he founded the monastery of Luxeuil in the Vosges mountains. But his success there and political unrest drove him over much of Europe until in the end he found peace at Bobbio in Italy where he died in 615.

St. Brendan's ship atop a curled-up fish, 15th century German illustration
(Universitätsbibliothek Heidelberg).

As trade between Ireland and England must have gone on simultaneously during all this time, the Irish Sea would seem to have been well traversed by these so typical skin-covered boats, and holy men and merchants must often have joined forces and travelled together.

Besides Columbanus, who is almost a symbol of the Irish church abroad, the best known Irish saint to voyage forth must be *St. Brendan.* St. Brendan the Navigator was born in Co. Kerry in 484 and was baptized by Bishop Erc of Kerry. *St. Ita*, the founder of a monastery in Munster, was his foster mother and first teacher. Later on he studied under *St. Jarlath* of Tuam and *St. Enda* of the Aran Islands. It appears that the young Brendan always had a liking for boats and the sea. He sailed his skin boat along the entire West coast of Ireland to the islands off Western Scotland and to Iona to meet St. Columcille. He even found time to sail to Wales to become abbot of the monastery of Llancarvon for a while. Perhaps he may even have reached the Faroes before finally setting off on his longest voyage. He sailed forth in search of the 'Land of Peace' promised by God to those who did His Will. With him were but a few companions. It is said, he never did find the land of peace, but many believe he reached America. After a number of years and many adventures St. Brendan returned to Ireland to live out his life at his monastery of Enach-Duin, (Annadown), where he died on May 16th in 577.

St. Brendan's 'Navigatio' is today the oldest surviving record of Christian monks travelling across the oceans. It was written sometime in the eleventh century and there are several versions. Quite probably the Navigatio was composed much earlier, perhaps even during St. Brendan's life-time. However, there is no claim in the manuscript that he was the first to sail via 'the Stepping Stones', the northern islands, to the Promised Land. The monk *St. Barrind* and *Abbot Mermoc* were recorded as having sailed that way before him. So frequent seem to have been these sea voyages, that the two masted skin boat, built of oak and ash and covered by oxhides must have been very sea-worthy indeed.

Tim Severin's "St. Brendan" in stormy Atlantic conditions *(Hunt Museums Trust)*.

In 1976 Tim Severin set out to prove or disprove the possibility of sailing such distances in these apparently so flimsy vessels. He built his 'St. Brendan' as an exact replica of a fifth or sixth century skin boat, following all the building instructions and using the same materials as recorded in St. Brendan's Navigatio. In the end he and his crew sailed successfully from the West coast of Ireland via the 'Stepping Stones' to America, proving to his satisfaction that St. Brendan and his crew of monks could have accomplished this almost a thousand years before Columbus and, four to five hundred years before the Viking Eric the Red rediscovered 'Vinland' or America.

St. Brendan's Day is still recognized in the Irish calendar on May 16th.

These seafaring holy men left a permanent mark wherever they went. Christianity, which had come to Ireland from across the sea, was in its turn spread from Ireland with renewed vigor back across the open seas by these monks who ventured forth in small and fragile skin-covered boats.

A German scholar, by name of Zimmer, is credited with having said when talking about the early Irish monks,... "They were the possessors and bearers of a higher culture than was to be found anywhere on the Continent," and he attributed to them the laying of the "corner-stone of western culture on the continent."

NOTE. (1) Island off the coast of Scotland.

CHAPTER 7

THE VIKINGS

795 - 1014.

So far we have seen that Ireland was settled first by mesolithic and then by neolithic people coming from across the sea. In turn Ireland had itself colonized parts of Scotland, Wales and England. It had traded across the waters, and its missionaries had travelled and Christianized large areas of the then known world. It was the longships of the Vikings, their 'langskips' which turned the tide and brought the men from the North raiding and plundering onto the Irish shores.

Many times there had been warnings of invaders and disasters, but they had remained unheeded. As early as the sixth century St. Bredan, whose death is given as 557 in the 'Annals of the Four Masters', had warned;

"Gentiles shall come over the soft sea;
They shall confound the men of Eirinn;
Of them there shall be an Abbot over every church;
Of them there shall be a king over Eirinn."

Again, one can read in a Welsh Chronicle of 790, the 'Brut y Tywysagion', the ominous statement: "10 years with fourscore and seven hundred was the age of Christ when the Pagans went to Ireland".

Although the Viking word 'langskip' derives from the Latin 'navis langa', the ship itself was developed and refined by the people of Scandinavia alone.

The earliest known Viking ship was found in a moor in Denmark, near Nydam in 1863, and dates from about 300 A.D. It had a rounded bottom, was 23 meters long, had oak planks and neither keel nor mast. About three hundred years later the Scandinavians invented the keel boat which was to revolutionize ship building and make their boats faster and much more sea-worthy than others. Though the saw was much used as a tool in Scandinavia as elsewhere, their shipwrights preferred the axe, splitting the long oak trees

24

Early Viking 'Ship' Coin
(Antikvarisk - Topografiska Arkivet, Stockholm).

lengthwise from the outside bark to the core. This gave the finished plank flexibility as well as strength. A typical Viking ship had a keel, was clinker built but without a deck, had a mast with a square sail, oars, a side rudder for steering and was usually just over twenty meters long.

Where possible, the keel was cut from a single oak tree, otherwise two pieces were cut at an angle so as to overlap, and then were secured by rivets.

The strakes which formed the sides of the ships were very carefully graded as to thickness. Those under the waterline and those directly above were of the same thickness, while the strake at the waterline itself as well as the ones through which the oars were passed were the thickest, except for the strong and often double gunwales. Caulking was achieved with animal hair or wool which had been dipped in tar.

The mast of pine or ash could be as tall as 11 meters and rested on crutches amidships when not in use.

The large square sail hung from a single yard-arm and was fastened to another at the base. In early reports this sail was either blue and red striped or just plain red.. Only the carvings on the Gotland stones show checkered sails. But all were woven in a double layer of thick wool.

Viking Coins
(Antikvarisk - Topografiska Arkivet, Stockholm).

The oars, again of pine or ash, went through closeable holes and were so graded in length that they touched the water at one and the same time.

Although they were only used as an auxiliary form of power and often solely in emergencies or for quick manoeuvrability, it was ever important that their angle in relation to the waterline was as flat as possible for their most efficient use. Consequently, the sides of warships were lower between the upsweep of the bow and stern than the sides of trading vessels which relied on sail alone.

The side rudder for steering was fastened to the starboard quarter and was very effective. It could easily be handled by one man.

All boats carried landing ramps and as the draught of the ship itself was exceedingly shallow, seldom more than a meter, the Vikings could land and disembark far up shallow rivers and even on harbourless sloping beaches, raid and make a rapid get-away.

Vikings disembarking by landing ramps (*after F. Moll*).

Having both sails and oars, their ships could outrun and out manoeuvre with ease the far clumsier sailing ships of the peoples they attacked. Their warships were troop carriers, not in themselves equipped to fight, the fighting men manned the oars and sail and no space was wasted on non-combat troops.

In old Norse law books one can read about the measuring of ships by 'rooms'. Each room was equal to a pair of oars. A normal boat could have twenty rooms, i.e. forty oars. The size of the boat could vary however, sometimes increasing up to thirty rooms. In one Norse saga one even hears of a sixty roomed vessel which would have been forty-nine meters in length.

"Dragonships" they were called in fear; their fearsome dragons heads on the bow and sometimes also the stern were elaborately carved and detachable. None was to be carried when the ships neared their homeland.

By about A.D. 1000, Viking ships had developed into four easily distinguishable types. The biggest by far were the **Drakar** or Dragonships, the Viking's warships which could carry up to three hundred men. The fastest, and by far the most versatile, were the **Langskips** or navis longa. They were build for speed and easy handling, could be thirty meters long and carry up to two hundred men. Much smaller and with an even more shallow draught was the **Karve**, an all purpose boat which was sometimes used for pleasure. Some twenty-one meters long with just sixteen oars or eight rooms. Only one design relied almost entirely on the sail, the **Knarr**. She was meant to travel safely across the oceans with her deep keel and higher sides. A cargo vessel, about fifteen meters long, she was able to carry a load of about 15,000 kilos, needing only a skeleton crew for easy handling. Speed varied with the design, but it has been found that a well built Viking ship could achieve a speed of up to ten knots.

The Danish historian Johannes Brondsted spoke truly and with feeling when he said of the Vikings and their vessels:

"The ships of the Vikings were the supreme achievement of their technical skill, the pinnacle of their material culture; they were the foundation of their power, their delight, and their most treasured possession. What the temple was to the Greeks, the ship was to the Vikings; the complete and harmonious expression of a rare ability."

Today we are able to view three great Norwegian Viking ships in the museum in Oslo. They were all buried with the owner and his

The Gokstad ship (Gokstadshipet), *(Universitetets Oldsaksamling, Oslo)*.

28

or her possessions in tumuli, two on the West coast and one on the East. The **Tune** ship, so called because it was found near Tune in Eastern Norway, was the first to be excavated, in 1867. She had originally been some twenty meters long and four meters wide, but was in bad condition and without decoration. Built of oak with a pine rudder she dates from about between A.D. 850 and 900. The next to be found, in 1880, was the **Gokstad** ship. She was well preserved, about twenty-three meters long and five meters wide and built of oak. She carried a big mast block and had sixty-four shields attached to her gunwales. Furthermore she had sixteen pairs of oars, a mast of pine and a three meter long oaken rudder. The Gokstad ship also contained a variety of beautiful grave goods as well as two smaller boats, elegantly built of thin oak planks. The last of the three ships to be excavated was the **Oseberg** ship, in 1904. She was more elegant, not so sea-worthy as the Gokstad with only twelve strakes and an overall length of twenty-one and a half meters and width of five meters, but well ornamented with lovely friezes along the prow ending high up in a carved snake's head. She too was built of oak with pine for the deck and some beech on the gunwale, carring fifteen pairs of rather short oars. Her grave goods were those belonging to the female side of the household, and included kitchen ware, sleds, a wagon and various chests.

A whole period of our history, almost three hundred years, is named after the invading and marauding people who came from across the waters in their beautiful yet fearsome boats. These Northmen, or Nordmanni, seem to have called themselves **Viking**, a word that probably came from the Norse word 'vikingr' which meant pirate or sea rover. A German ecclesiastical historian, Adam of Bremen, wrote in 1075... "The pirates whom they - the Danes - call Vikings but we - the Germans - call Ashmen..."; Ashmen or Ascomanni because ash trees were used in the building of their boats. In Irish literature they appear as **Gall** or **Ghoill** - stranger - or **Lochlannach** - northerner - and sometimes bear the added **Finn** or **Finn Ghoill** for fair stranger or Norwegian and **Dubh** or **Dubh Ghoill** for dark stranger or Dane. The reasons for this division are uncertain. Some say it followed the colour of their shields and others because the Norwegians were tall and fair and the Danes seemed to be shorter and darker. Fair or dark, the fear they evoked was real enough and equally strong.

There was at that time a High King at Tara with seven lesser kindoms which bore submission to him. These were Connacht, Munster, Leinster, Meath, Ailech, Ulaidh and Oriel. All of these struggled amongst themselves for supremacy and as a consequence they were quite unable to present a united front and repell the invaders. To the Vikings Ireland was a country full of gold, art and learning, a mild green haven with a divided populace who were quite unwilling or incapable of defending themselves against an even numerically inferior force, yet one whose mobility on the water was surprising and horrifying.

Why did these strangers suddenly appear on Ireland's shores? In the seventh and eighth centuries there was hunger in Scandinavia due to over-population and wasteful farming practices. Polygamy was widely practised yet their laws of inheritance remained those of primogeniture. This in turn left many young men free to roam and seek their fortunes beyond the shores of their homelands. Internal struggle was widespread and piracy and trade occupied much of the restless population. One Olaus Wormius once said (and was so quoted by Sir James Ware in 1654):

"Piracy was among the Danes, Honourable and Lawful, and Kings themselves and their children, with the most Valiant and Notorious they could find, addicted themselves that way."

Vikings believed in a glorious afterlife in Valhalla, their heaven, if killed in a good fight.

"A King is for Glory not for long Life",
the Viking Magnus Bareleg is supposed to have shouted as he engaged in a fight in Ireland.

The first recorded Viking raid was on June 8th in 793 A.D. against the monastery on Lindisfarne off the East Coast of England.

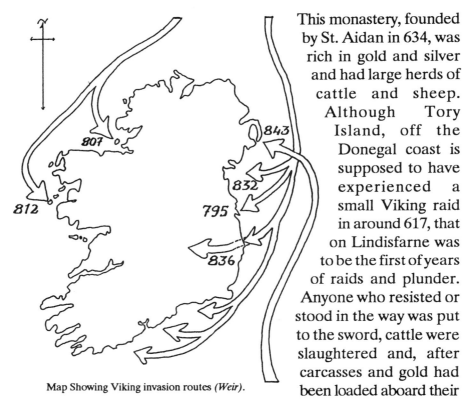

Map Showing Viking invasion routes *(Weir)*.

This monastery, founded by St. Aidan in 634, was rich in gold and silver and had large herds of cattle and sheep. Although Tory Island, off the Donegal coast is supposed to have experienced a small Viking raid in around 617, that on Lindisfarne was to be the first of years of raids and plunder. Anyone who resisted or stood in the way was put to the sword, cattle were slaughtered and, after carcasses and gold had been loaded aboard their ships, the Vikings set fire to the buildings and sailed away. The news of this success must have spread across Scandinavia because the raids increased in the following year. By 795 the Viking dragonships appeared off Ireland at Rechru, now called Lambay Island off Howth, and sacked it. More and more Vikings followed. In 807 Inishmurry Island was raided twice and burned. In 812 the Vikings appeared off the Connemara coast and slew the local inhabitants. The Annals of Ulster record at this time:

"The sea spewd forth floods of foreigners over Erin, so that no haven, no landing place, no stronghold, no fort, no castle might be found, but it was submerged by waves of vikings and pirates;"

And yet it has also been recorded, that during this same time the Irish raided amongst themselves with a terrifying frequency. By

31

832 the Viking raids had become more organized and were on a larger scale and the first small settlements were started, to the point where by the middle of the ninth century they had even established a monarchy of Dublin.

One of St. Columcille's prophesies is recorded in the book of Leinster as a quatrain:

"Those ships upon Loch Ree,
Well do they magnify the pagan foreigners;
They will give an Abbot to Ardmacha;
His rule will be the rule of a tyrant."

Ardmacha was the name for the modern Armagh.

Dublin, once a small Celtic settlement called ATH CLIATH, Ford of the Hurdles, after the wicker bridge which spanned the Liffey where the road from Royal Tara met the river, was occupied by Turgesius the Norwegian in 836. By 840 he was powerful enough to fortify Dublin and not only to raid the countryside but also turn the town into a prosperous trading centre, sending his merchant ships to faraway countries. They carried hides, wool, grain, timber, fish and golden vessels from Ireland and returned with salt, metals and wine from France and Spain, as well as spices and precious silks which had been brought over long trading routes from the Far East. Turgesius and his Norwegians called their new settlement DYFLIN, changing the Irish word DUBHLINN, meaning Black Pool, to suit their own tongue. From here and Armagh, where he made himself Abbot, he ruled, killed and raided for thirteen years. His death was vividly described in 1704 by Sir James Ware who had translated the much simpler story related in Cambrensis's 'Topographia Hiberniae':

"In the year 845, the Norwegians Plunder'd and Burn'd Clonmacnois, Clonfert, Lochran and Tirdaglass. Likewise about the same year Turgesius fell in love with the Daughter of Melachlin (variously also called Melfechlin or Murchard Ua Maelechlainn or Omachlachelinus) King of Meath, and the King with a Malicious intention granted him his daughter, and promis'd to send her to an Island of Meath, viz. the Isle of Lochwair (today Loch Owel) with 15 other beautiful Maids: Turgesius well satisfied, came to the place appointed with the like number of his Nobility, and found in the island 15 beardless Young Men, chosen out for the purpose, and clad in womens apparel, who under that Habit conceal'd their Arms, with which they treated Turgesius instead of the embraces which he expected, and he was there killed with the rest of his company."

After his death the Norsemen temporarily lost much of their power over the Irish, though they still raided and even kept fleets of ships on many of the major Irish lakes enabling them to reach almost any part of the country with a minimum of delay.

It was now the turn of the Danes. Arriving from the South, and much

King Olaf crossing Stormy sea *(from a 14th century Danish Church mural).*

better organized, they appeared for the first time in 843 and then again in the following year. By 850 they were established in

Carlingford from where they attacked Dublin in 851. At first the Irish, hoping at long last to expell the hated Finn Ghoill, sided with the Danes. But soon the old squabbles arose again and the Norwegians remained in possession of most of their other towns and settlements.

Just two years later, in 853, Olaf, son of Lochlann of Norway arrived and again ousted the Danes from Dublin. For almost twenty years the city remained his Irish capital. As Aulaff the White, he was also king of Northumbria with York as his capital. The trading connection he established between these two cities was to last for nearly a century. His brothers Sitric and Ivar founded the towns of Waterford and Limerick respectively. When Olaf died in a battle in Norway in 871, Ivar succeeded him for a short time, styling himself 'Rex Nordmannorum Totius Hiberniae et Britanniae'. (King of the Norsemen and over all of Ireland and Britain).

Vikings kept coming but were also departing from Irish shores for further exploration to the West. By now they had established five major trading centres in Ireland: Dublin, Cork, Waterford, Wexford and Limerick. Although at all times their supremacy was almost exclusively centered on these coastal sites, their raids continued to harass the Irish and their trade carried them and Irish goods far and wide. Irish objects have been discovered in archaeological digs at all major sites in Scandinavia. Among them was the head of an ornate crozier at Helgoe, and in Germany a gold plated bronze buckle was found at Haithabu, the modern Hedeby in Schleswig Holstein, where in the 1960s archaeologists also excavated a fine Viking ship. Not only goods but also slaves were traded by the Vikings; it is recorded that one Viking slave dealer named 'Gille the Russian', from his habit of wearing Russian fur caps, specialized in Irish girls whom he sold in the market of what is now Goeteborg in Sweden. From around 995 the Dublin Vikings even minted their own coins.

By the end of the tenth century the Irish High King, Malachy II, was finally able to inflict many defeats on the Vikings and so weaken their power. But it fell to Brian Boru (Brian Borumha or

Brian Boroimhe) king of the Dalcassians, perhaps the one and only king able to rule all of Ireland as a true Ard Ri, to defeat the Vikings conclusively at the battle of Clontarf in 1014, only to be slain himself the same day.

The Battle of Clontarf, A. D. 1014.

Following this defeat the remaining Vikings became absorbed into Irish life although they remained primarily in the vicinity of their traditional coastal centres.

Almost three hundred years of Viking domination left Ireland and the Irish very changed. Although robbed of many of their treasures, they had gained in other ways. Formerly a pastoral society, they were now brought into contact with widespread trade and urban life. Irish curraghs virtually disappeared from the high seas, to be replaced by the new wooden-planked boats. The curragh, then as now survived only on the wild and rugged West coast. Many Viking nautical and trade words became part of the Irish, and later on English, languages, such as:

The Viking, a copy of the Gokstad ship, sailed by Magnus Andersen in 1893 from Norway to Chicago, Illinois *(Viking Ship Restoration Committee, Evanston).*

berlingr-- bharra -- boom
segl -- seol -- sail
popta -- tochta -- thwart
margard -- margadh -- market
kjoll -- cile -- keel
stag -- scriuta -- stay
styri -- ram stiurtha -- steering oar
pingin -- pingin -- penny
and many more.

Old tribal customs were no longer sacred institutions and the Celtic Church, which had been organized around the great monasteries, changed rapidly, moving closer to the Roman Church and away from its Brehon influences.

Lately, Viking ships and ship designing have tempted modern sailors to build copies and sail them to try out their sea-worthiness. A copy of the Gokstad ship in the Oslo museum was successfully sailed across the Atlantic ocean in 1893 by the Norwegian Magnus Andersen. It was shown at the World Fair in Chicago that year, and is still housed in a special building in a city park. Again, almost a century later, in October of 1984, another Norwegian, Ragnar Thorseth, sailed a copy of a Knarr, which he named 'Saga Siglar', Sailor of the Seas, from Norway to Chicago from where he planned to sail her on and eventually circumnavigate the globe. This he did successfully.

CHAPTER 8

THE NORMANS 1169 - 13th CENTURY.

In 1881 Charles Haliday wrote in his 'The Scandinavian Kingdom of Dublin': "... Consequently in all our annals of intestine warfare, although we have records of the destruction of Armagh and Clonmacnois, of Emania and Aileach (Elagh in Co. Donegal) and of duns, fortresses and fastnesses, there is no allusion to the siege of an Irish town, or the destruction of an Irish city. And not only is there no Irish record of a 'City of Dublin' before the 9th century; but before that period there is no record that the place where the city now stands was the place of any importance. Our annals refer to the Dubhlinn or harbour, which was the resort of ships, and to Ath Cliath, or bridge of hurdles, which crossed the river; but if there were a dun or rath near the harbour, that fortress never was the seat of an Irish king, the capital of an Irish territory, or the centre of Irish dominion; and as regards the present metropolitan supremacy of Dublin, it is manifest that Henry the Second made Dublin the metropolis of his royalty, not because he considered it to be the

Henry II
(Screen statue in York Cathedral).

capital of Ireland (over which he claimed a "lordship"), or because its

38

position was more advantageous than that either of Wexford or Waterford (then the ports of communication with England), but because it was the principal city of the Ostmen he had conquered, and over whose subjugated territories he did claim to exercise regal privileges.... it thence became the capital of his Irish dominion and from the extension of that dominion it has become the capital of Ireland".

The Normans, themselves of Viking stock, officially invaded Ireland for the first time on St. Luke's day (October 18th) of 1171. In reality, however, the first Norman troops had landed in Ireland two years earlier, in May 1169.

As one can see on the Bayeux tapestry, the Normans' boats were essentially still the Viking ships with which their ancestors had landed in Normandy. They still used the side rudder and large square sail. No oars are shown in use, yet some of the smaller boats seem to have oar holes just below the gunwale.

Like so many events which ultimately change the face of a nation, the Norman invasion of Ireland came about through a local incident. Diarmuid MacMurrough, King of Leinster, had fallen in love with the wife of Tighernan O'Rourke and had abducted her. He therefore had to flee from the vengeful O'Rourke. He sailed to Wales to try to persuade Henry II and his barons to help him regain his territories in Ireland. Although Henry promised his help, he was himself preoccupied with other matters and did not act immediately, but gave leave to Diarmuid to enlist the assistance of any who might wish to follow him.

So, by May 1169, Diarmuid crossed to Ireland with three boats containing an efficient force of thirty knights in full armour, sixty horsemen in half armour and some three hundred archers. They landed at Bannow in Co. Wexford. With him were the knights Robert Fitz Stephen, Herve de Mon Maurice (**Montorency ??**), Robert de Barry, Meiler Fitz Henry and 'a horde of fighting Flemings'. Less than a month later, two more boats crossed the Irish Sea with some two hundred archers under Maurice de Prendergast. These

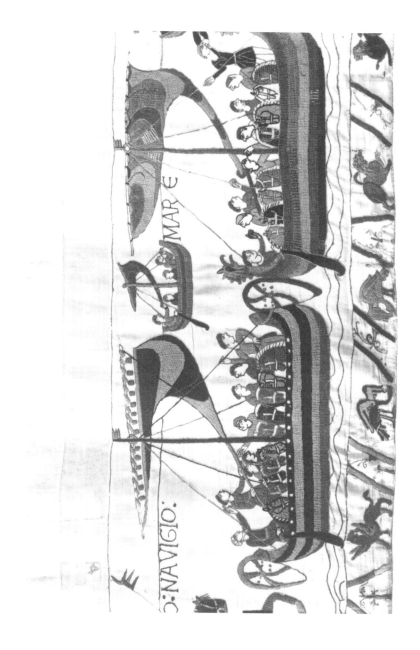

Tapiserie de Bayeux (Bayeux Tapestry), XI° siècle (avec autorisation spéciale de la Ville de Bayeux).

two forces combined and together took Wexford. When Maurice Fitz Gerald landed with another force of archers, horsemen and knights that autumn, they marched towards Dublin and gained the submission of its people. Early 1170 saw more boats crossing from Wales with fighting men. This group was led by Raymond Fitz Gerald, who landed his troops at Dundonnell. Then in August of the same year Strongbow (Richard de Clare, Earl of Pembroke) followed with a force of two hundred knights and a thousand additional troops and landed at

Ireland when the Normans came *(Weir)*.

Crook near Waterford. Together they ransacked Waterford and Dublin, and subjugated much of Wexford, Meath and Breffni (Cavan).

Now Henry saw the need to cross over to Ireland himself, to show his barons who was master and to lay claim to his sovereignty over the Emerald Isle. It was the custom of the Normans at that time to rely heavily on their archers when fighting. For this reason they preferred autumn campaigns when the leaves had fallen from the trees and there was good visibility. Fifteen per cent of Ireland was still wooded at this time and the Irish, according to the contemporary historian Giraldus Cambrensis ".... pay no regard to castles, but use the woods as their strongholds and the marshes as their entrenchments." Consequently Henry prepared to visit in October and arrived at

Crook on October 8th 1171 with an awe-inspiring fleet of four hundred boats holding some four thousand troops and five hundred knights. He achieved both his goals; many Irish chiefs submitted to him including The O'Brien, The MacCarthy and The O'Rourke and his own barons acknowledged his authority. It was not long before the Ard Ri and the Bishops also swore their fealty.

Within a year the Normans were securely installed and although the fighting continued sporadically, they were here to stay and consolidate their power.

Duvelina, the latinized form of the Viking Dyflin, became the capital of Norman Ireland. But, inspite of all their success, power and strongholds, even the Normans never really conquered it. The country lacked a centralized authority, and with no true national monarchy, no single ruler's defeat could ever mean the defeat of the whole island, as it had in England after Harold's defeat at Hastings in 1066 when virtually the whole country fell to the Normans.

Once again, as during the height of the Viking period, there was a constant coming and going across the sea as more and more Norman settlers followed to stay in Ireland.

Seal of Winchelsea, 13th century.

CHAPTER 9

BRUCE INVASION 1315 - 1318.

Ship development continued although there were no major breakthroughs during the next two hundred years.

By the early fourteenth century, most northern European ships had a straight stem and stern thus improving the boats' overall strength and sailing ability. The Hanseatic Cog is a good example, though it was, strictly speaking, primarily a trading vessel and few of them were used by the Irish or English. This cog was still clinker-built and had a high freeboard, making it almost impregnable. The oars and oar holes were gone, as was the steering oar. There was now a stern rudder Fore and aft were high decks from which a bowman could easily aim at the much lower longships. The Scandinavians and English were loath to lose the superior speed and manoeuvrability of their longships and tried to raise castles fore and aft, and sometimes even on the mast itself so that their bowmen could attack the much slower cogs. The owners of cogs simply raised their decks and thereby remained superior in defence. However, many English coast-hugging vessels retained the rounded stem and stern.

It was probably on such latter boats that Edward Bruce, brother of the Scottish king, Robert the Bruce, invaded Ireland on 16th May, 1315 with a force of some six thousand men.

The harsh Norman rule had made many Irish chiefs realize that unity amongst themselves was needed if they were ever to regain supremacy over their country. In 1263 some even went so far as to offer the Irish crown to Norway's King Haakon, but these plans were terminated by his untimely death.

During all the long conflict between England and Scotland, the Irish were forced to supply men for the English armies. Robert the Bruce had once been in Ireland, when fleeing from his enemies in 1294, and had probably stayed on Rathlin Island. So when he gained his decisive victory over the English at the battle of Bannockburn in

June 1314, the thought of sending his restless brother Edward to Ireland to fight the English on Irish soil presented itself easily. Therefore when Edward landed at Carrigfergus he was warmly received by The O'Neill, The O'Hanlon, The McCarton and The O'Hagan. Donnell O'Neill, King of Ulster, and other princes even wrote to the Holy See to explain why they were now offering the crown of Ireland to Edward Bruce. They mentioned the cruelties of the English and the injustices in the application of their laws.

Meanwhile, Edward with his army and their supporters marched, plundered and burned their way south and west, meeting no real resistance except at Dublin which they simply circumvented. A year later, in Ulster, Edward was crowned King of Ireland. For a short while King Robert himself crossed the Irish Sea with a supporting army, and together they marched and ravaged the Irish countryside. The rest of Ireland, seeing only destruction all around them, took up their own quarrels again and, taking various sides at different times, left the country to the mercy of the Scots. By the end of May 1317, Robert had to return to Scotland leaving his brother to continue alone. Finally on 14th November, 1318 Edward, without having achieved anything positive, was slain in a battle near Dundalk by one John Maupas who fought with the Normans under Lord John de Bermingham.

Three and a half years of murder, plunder, war and famine left Ireland in poverty and utter confusion with the English settlers once more trying to gain the upper hand.

CHAPTER 10

THE SPANISH ARMADA 1588.

A three - masted Carrack.

Great changes took place in shipbuilding during the early fifteenth century and thereafter. The single-masted ship with its one large square sail, which hitherto had dominated the ship building traditions of Northern Europe, was slowly being replaced by three-masted vessels. The clinker-built hulls were also being replaced by carvel-built ships, that is, the planks were no longer overlapping but laid edge to edge, thus enabling the builder to use far heavier planks and eventually to built much larger ships better able to cross the oceans.

An early single - masted Carrack.

The first of this new type of ship to come out of the Mediterranean and sail in Northern waters was the **Carrack**. The vessel itself was rather clumsy, originally built as a merchant ship and only afterwards converted into a fighting vessel carrying mounted guns and with room for archers and spear throwers at the top of the masts. The carrack had the new three-mast design, a strong mainmast with a square sail, another square sail on the foremast and a lateen-rigged mizzenmast. This latter sail enabled the ship to sail somewhat into the wind and even to tack. At times all three masts also carried small topsails. The carrack's sides were reinforced and the ship had high fighting platforms.

The high castle in front often protuded well beyond the bow line while the platform in the stern now had two decks, frequently covered by an awning. These towering platforms were designed for hand to hand fighting and for boarding hostile vessels, but being so high, they acted like a sail, so that the winds thrust the ship to leewards. This effect necessitated a deep keel and the use of ever larger mizzensails and foresails. However, with the introduction of artillery, the high castles disappeared and moved well within the bowline. The carrack was doomed nevertheless, and replaced by the faster and handier **Galleon** which in comparison looked almost like a racing yacht.

The origin of the Spanish **Galleon** is somewhat obscure, yet once started it developed quickly and its design spread northwards. Unlike the galley and galleas, the galleon carried no oars and relied solely on its sails for propulsion. In fact a large galleon often had four masts carrying the usual square sails as well as smaller lateen sails. The galleon was also much slimmer than the carrack it replaced, with the forecastle much lower and well within the bowline. In time a so-called beakhead was developed, being almost a continuation of the foredeck and designed to keep the low forecastle as dry as possible in heavy seas. The stern castle, being much higher, was used as the bridge, thus providing an almost uninterrupted view ahead. The galleon's several decks were often fashioned of beautifully carved and decorated wood. Another new feature was the gunports on two or more decks, yet the range of the cannons on even the largest Spanish galleon was not more than a hundred and fifty meters and

A Galleon.

they were quite ineffectual at three hundred. With all its beauty and apparent efficiency, the Spanish galleon was yet an unwieldy vessel by modern standards. The English galleon on the other hand, although evolved from the Spanish proto-type, was by the beginning of the sixteenth century somewhat lower in the stern and altogether longer and narrower, allowing superior manoeuvrability.

The other, smaller vessels emerging from the South were the **Galley** and the **Galleas**.

The **Galley** had evolved from the early Mediterranean tireme with its many oars and oarsmen. But whereas there had been two or three tiers of oars arranged along either side of the ship, each oar operated by one man, now there were larger single oars each manned by more

A Galleas.

than one person. Besides oars, a sixteenth century galley often had one or even three masts with the mainmast carrying either a square or lateen sail. The galley also had small decks fore and aft and was capable of carrying several guns. It still had a remnant of the old ram but this was now above the waterline. In waters where there was often little wind between storms, such as the Mediterranean, a galley had the great advantage of fast manoeuvrability because of its oar power.

The **Galleas** on the other hand had been an attempt to retain the strength of a carrack and combine it with the manoeuverability of the galley. Thus it kept the oars of the latter in addition to three masts with lateen rigging, and carried heavy guns on fore and aft decks as well as the usual lighter ones. Many still had a ram below the water line, perhaps retained for its original purpose of ramming an opponent's vessel. However, as the galleas was rather low in the water, it was disadvantaged in the heavy seas and strong winds of the Northern waters. Even though only one of the four galleasses with the Spanish Armada was actually lost on the Irish coast, they were never really favoured by northern sailors.

The smaller sailing vessels, which the English called Pinnaces, and the Spanish, Pataches and Zabras, were used successfully by all countries along their coast lines; they were, however, unsuitable for longer ocean voyages.

These, the carrack, galleon, galley and galleas were the most effective warships on European waters when the Spanish Armada sailed towards England, and to its final doom on the Irish coast, in the latter part of the sixteenth century.

The last two centuries had seen an outward quiet in Ireland, producing no major foreign invasions or any great destruction. True, there had been rebellions, which were suppressed with great cruelty; foreign ships had landed in hope of help or offering help, but mainly the English had kept to themselves in the Pale and their other strongholds. Especially in the North and West, the Irish were left alone, or as much as the English thought safe.

When Sir William Fitzwilliam took office as the Lord Deputy of Ireland in 1588, he was almost immediately confronted with the news of Spanish ships being sighted off the Irish coast.

The English had been well aware of the imminent arrival of the great Spanish Armada. What they feared most, and had been afraid of for a long time, was the possibility of a Spanish landing on the Irish coast and thus of an alliance of Spanish and Irish forces in order to drive out the English from Ireland, followed by an attack on England itself from a strong Irish position. On Irish soil, England had but a small force of soldiers with poor equipment and could scarcely afford to increase it. They also knew of the many Irish who had fled their oppression and religious persecution and who were now residing in Spain under the protection of His Most Catholic Majesty, Philip II, constantly trying to enlist his help to free their homeland from her English overlord. As it turned out, the magnificent Spanish Armada sailed under different orders, straight for England.

Philip of Spain, a fanatic defender of the Catholic faith felt it his duty to free England from the Protestant yoke, quite aside from the fact that the English were a thorn in his side in other ways. Drake not only preyed on his 'Plate Fleet' from the Americas but had also attacked the city of Cadiz in the South of Spain, and had burned valuable cargoes. Besides, England continued to send aid to the Netherlands to help them in their own fight against Philip. To put an end to all these troubles, Philip set about equipping the biggest fleet ever assembled under one flag.

When the Armada finally left Lisbon in May of 1588 under the command of the Duke of Medina Sidonia, it comprised some one hundred and twenty eight vessels and almost thirty thousand men. Almost at once they were beset by foul weather and contrary winds and had to take refuge in Corunna. From here in July with fresh supplies, the Armada once again set off.

The Duke of Medina Sidonia, an able soldier but one who neither understood nor liked the sea, had been given orders to sail into the English channel and from there to act as convoy and protector to the Duke of Parma who was assembling troops in the Netherlands for an invasion of England. Only after accomplishing this was he to engage the English Navy. He was warned of the superior fire power of the English and advised to stay in formation at all times. By now the Armada consisted of some one hundred and thirty ships, mostly galleons and merchantmen, with additonal hulks for stores, pataches and zabras and four each of galleys and galleasses. On arrival in the English channel, they found the Duke of Parma not yet fully prepared to embark his forces. But the English Navy was waiting and when the winds changed in its favour, not even the tight crescent shaped battle formation of the Armada could withstand the superior fire power and cunning of the English. By August 9th, it was all over. The Armada was scattered, their most valuable anchors cut off in the haste to avoid the advancing and dreaded fire ships. Their shot and supplies were low, and many ships were badly damaged. They then decided to sail north around Scotland and out into the open Atlantic before turning South West for a safe run back to Spain. In his final orders to the fleet, the Duke of Medina Sidonia warned:

"Take care not to fall upon the coast of Ireland because of the harm that may come to you there."

Had he heard of the dangers of the Irish coastline? Although there had been regular trade by sea between Spain and Ireland since early times neither country knew much of the coastline of the other. They had exchanged goods such as fish, hides, fur, timber, linen and wine, and Spanish fishing fleets, then as now, had come to fish on the rich Irish banks offshore. Indeed, in 1572 one Sir Humphrey Gibberd had reported more than six hundred Spanish fishing vessels off the Irish coast. The sailors knew only those ports with which they traded and the coastline, especially north of Galway, was virtually undiscovered by them. This coast is still wild and rugged and dangerous to those sailing along it without adequate charts and tide tables. There are countless bays and inlets with rocks and submerged reefs; strong currents swirl back and forth, at times producing local cross currents to add to the difficulties. Over forty Irishmen, possibly many more, are known to have sailed with the Armada, yet none seems to have been able to avert the coming disaster.

Those ships which followed Medina Sidonia's advice and which were able to sail far out to sea before turning towards Spain eventually reached their homeland, or sank, but none were wrecked. The reasons that so many sailed towards the Irish shore were quite involuntary. Starting on August 21st, there were two weeks of constant fog, rain and gales out of the South-West. As the Queen's clerk for the council of Connacht, Edward Whyte, wrote:

"There has blown a most extreme wind and cruel storm, the like whereof hath not been seen or heard for a long time."

The ships were over-crowded, with little or no sanitation, and the crews were ill with dysentery. The food supply, what little there was left, was rotten and infested with worms. The drinking water had run out days before, or was too foul for consumption. Sailors and soldiers died in ever increasing numbers. The ships themselves were in no better state. Several of them were badly shot up, the already weakened rigging broke in the heavy winds, top-heavy masts made the ships keel over, or were so shot through that they could no longer support the heavy sails. The water inside the tossing vessels was rising as the seams in the planking widened and weakened crews could no longer cope with the pumps. Many of them when sighting land, had but one thought; to forsake these rapidly deteriorating vessels. In their haste they hit submerged rocks without ever having seen them. As the Spanish historian F. Duro later wrote:

"They were lost, partly from bad pilotage, partly from bad seamanship, but chiefly becasue they were leaking like sieves, had no anchors, their masts and rigging were shattered and their watercasks were smashed."

Headwinds were a sixteenth centuy sailor's nightmare, and the wind was blowing out of the South-West. Most of the ships in the Armada were square rigged which made sailing into the wind impossible. A sailor had two choices when confronted with a heavy head wind; he could furl his sails and let the ship drift until weather conditions changed, or he could attempt to tack. Both alternatives needed a great deal of seaspace and the fear of being wrecked was ever present.

On September 5th and 15th the first big ships were sighted from Ireland, off the Sligo coast and off Co. Clare, then a part of Connacht. There followed a rush of sightings and reports of ships coasting along or already wrecked and broken up. It was then that the fearful Lord Deputy wrote:

"We have neither men, money nor munition to answer these extraordinary services..." and later again:

"We look rather to be over-run by the Spaniards than otherwise..."

On September 18th he himself received a note from the governor of Connacht, Sir Richard Bingham, stating:

"Even now I received the enclosed letter from the Sheriff of Thomond, by which your Lordship shall perceive some further news of strange ships; whether they be of the dispersed fleet which are fled from the supposed overthrow in the Narrow Seas, or new forces come from Spain directly, no man is able to advertise otherwise than by guess, which does rather show their coming from Spain,.... by all likelyhoods they mind to land."

Here again, plain to see, was the fear of invading Spaniards who might ally themselves with the Irish and support their causes. The word went out, to capture and put to the sword any and all Spaniards who came ashore.

The landing of so large a force of Spaniards created problems not only for the English who knew their duty, but also for the Irish themselves. Many Irish had sworn fealty to the English Queen and so were duty-bound to obey the orders of her deputies. But for those who had known and traded with the Spaniards, had friends and even family among them and who shared their religion, the decisions were more complex, and fear of reprisals played not a small role. Yet there were those who did aid the straggling survivors, hid them in their castles, cottages and woods and helped them in their escape via Scotland to the continent. Included was The O'Rourke of Breffni,

The McSweeney and McDonnell of Antrim, The O'Neill, MacClancy, O'Cahan, O'Dogherty and the Bishop of Derry, Raymond Gallagher; all these and others, still being relatively free Irish chiefs, felt it their duty to shelter and aid the Spaniards. Later many had to pay with their own lives for their humanitarian actions. Still there were others, those in remote coastal districts, who had never before seen a stranger nor communicated with one. From ignorance and greed, they robbed the few survivors, killed them or abandoned them to the elements out of fear of the unknown. Amongst them, it was considered bad luck to save a drowning man. Should one do so, the superstition ran, oneself or any of ones family might be taken instead. This belief was not solely restricted to the West coast of Ireland, but was also held in Scotland, the Orkney Islands and amongst some African tribes. The Sea God Lir demanded his due.

Once, in earlier centuries, the old Brehon laws had made special provision for wrecked ships and stranded sailors. Then, a totally wrecked vessel became the legal property of the owner of the shoreline where it lay stranded. If it was above a certain value, measured in cows as was the custom, only some of the wreckage went to the local owner; the rest was divided between the king and the leading families of the area. A stranded sailor was to be lodged and fed as long as necessary "....for the district on whose shore the vessel is cast, is bound to keep, protect, feed, and make provision for such parties...." But the Brehon laws had been supplanted by English laws and were now quite forgotten.

From the day when the first Spanish ship, the Trinidad Valencera, was wrecked on the Irish coast in mid September, to the day the last ship lay stranded on the shore, was a mere six weeks. Twenty six ships, a quarter of the entire Spanish Armada, thus lay in wreckage along the Irish coast. The threat to English rule over Irelnd had passed. A delighted Sir Richard Bingham could write:

"....The Spaniards have departed, leaving but a few begging sick men..." And even these were hunted down and put to the sword.

He continues:

"Thus, having made a clear despatch of them, we rested Sunday all day, giving thanks to Almighty God for her Majesty's most happy success and deliverance from her most dangerous enemies...."

A scant seven hundred or so survivors managed to return to Spain from Ireland. In another few weeks the exitement over the once great Armada was gone, the last chance for the Irish chiefs to unite and drive out the English oppressor was lost for ever.

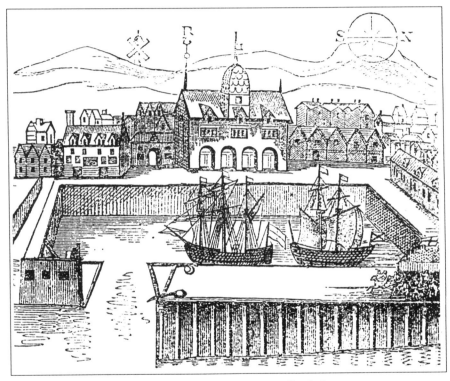

An early view of Youghal Harbour, Co. Cork.

CHAPTER 11

SHIPS AND IRISH CITIES AND FAMILIES.

A number of towns and families throughout Ireland carry ships on their seals or coats of arms to this day, indicating their long and constant involvement with boats. These are but an outward sign of the certainty that Ireland, as an island in a vast and often hostile sea, depended, then as now, on ships and those who would sail them.

There are six major sea-ports around the coast of Ireland which have traditionally carried such a ship on their town seal.

Galway, on the West coast, has been inhabited for a very long time and was first mentioned by Ptolemy in the second century who called it 'Nagnata or Naguata'. One of Galway's old Irish names

Galway.

seems to have been 'Cuan-na-Guactie' i.e 'Port of the Small Islands', a very apt description as not only the Aran islands lie in the adjoining bay but there are also a number of other small islands. As the area around Galway used to be called 'Clanfirgail' or 'the land (habitation) of the Gail or merchants', also referred to as 'Port-na-Gall', it probably indicated that the name 'Galway' derived from either of these. The word Gail or Gall meaning stranger shows the early connection, through trade, of Galway with the outside world. The town played no small role during the Viking era but mainly as a point of departure for their western explorations. It continued to remain an important trading centre well into this century when the area around the harbour became more quiet. Today a few merchant vessels, a sizeable fishing fleet and pleasure craft frequent this West coast harbour.

Cork, in the South of Ireland and the second largest city of the country today, was originally called 'Corach or Corach-Brecoin' i.e. 'a marshy place', originating from its position on the river Lee. Around 600 A.D., St. Finbar built a church, prior to his departure for England, and a settlement grew up around it. The Vikings too settled there, mainly on an island in the river close by. Dermot MacCarty, who held Cork under them was the first Irish chief to submit and pay homage to England's King Henry II on his arrival in Ireland in 1171. The fortunes of the town

Cork.

underwent many changes, but always there was trade especially with the Continent and the Mediterranean. Today it still has a busy harbour, and many visitors to Ireland first step ashore on its quays.

Further East, yet still on the Southern shore, lies **Youghal** at the confluence of the rivers Blackwater and Toragh. It derived its name, meaning 'a Wooded Place', from its location at the foot of a range of the, at that time, densely wooded hills. Youghal received its first charter of incorporation as early as 1209 from King John. Although its harbour must at all times have seen some trade, it seems to have been primarily a much used landing place for armed forces, be they Irish or foreign.

Youghal.

Following the coastline to the East, one comes upon **Waterford.** Its ancient Irish name seems to have been 'Cuan-na-Groith or Grian' signifying 'the Haven of the Sun', but later it obtained the name 'Gleann-na-Gleodh' i.e. 'the Valley of Lamentation', after a fight between the native Irish and the invading Vikings. Its modern name

Waterford.

derives from the Viking word 'Vader-Fiord' or 'the Ford of the Father'. The town as such was founded by Sitric, brother of Olaf, son of Lochlann of Norway, who ruled in Dublin from 853 A.D. for some twenty years. Due to its situation and importance, Waterford became the centre of communication and trade with England.

Dublin, the capital of Ireland, lies at the mouth of the Liffey half way along the East coast. Ptolemy was the first to mention this place, which he called Eblana. One of its first Irish names was 'Drom-Col-Coille' or 'the Hill of

Hazel Wood' from the number of these trees then growing on the high land. The next name was 'Baille-Ath-Cliath-Dubhlinne' meaning 'the Town of the Ford of Hurdles over the Black Pool' in the river Liffey. Besides these names, there is no further record of Dublin until 448 when, according to Joscelin, the then king of the area was baptised by St. Patrick. It remained a small

Dublin.

Celtic settlement until Turgesius the Norwegian arrived with a fleet of longships in 836 and made it his headquarters and a prosperous trading centre. The Norwegians called it 'Dyflin' after the former Dubhlinn. It was Henry II who changed the name to 'Duvelina' and from a combination of all of these, our modern name 'Dublin' finally evolved as being the prominent one. Dublin saw many conquerors and experienced much destruction, but always it grew and prospered, mainly due to the merchant fleets that were attracted by its good harbour facilities.

The Northern-most east coast town to have traditionally borne a ship on its seal, is **Carlingford**. There seems to be no ancient name for this town, even though some sources mention that St. Patrick landed here in 432. In 850 the Danes established a longphort, (a harbour for their longships), from which they raided the countryside and attacked Dublin. The town itself was started when King John ordered the construction of a castle in 1210. Today, as then, trade continues to flourish as well as an ever increasing fishing and fish rearing industry.

Carlingford.

Ennis.

Another town which bears ships on its seal is **Ennis,** the county town of Clare which is situated on the Fergus, an esturial tributary of the Shannon and which from medieval times had a trading tradition.

Of the many Irish families carrying a ship on their coat of arms, only a few shall be mentioned here. Almost all of them come from maritime counties and many have been involved in trade or other sea borne activities.

The O'Malleys from Co. Mayo not only lived along the Atlantic coast, but also carried on a far-flung sea trade as well as other maritime exploits. "Terra Marique Potens" [powerful on land and sea] is their motto.

The O'Flahertys hail from Co. Galway. There they were in command of a large area mainly west of the city, had many strongholds and a large fleet.

O'Malley

58

Meyers.

O'Driscoll.

O'Halloran.

MacDonnell of Clare.

Counties Galway and Clare were the homeland of the O'Hallorans while the O'Meroir [Meyers] sept came from Co. Clare alone.

Co. Cork was the territory of two great septs, the O'Driscolls and the O'Learys, both of which still have many descendants in that county.

O'Flaherty

O'Leary.

MacSheehy.

The powerful McDonnells of Co. Antrim were relative latecomeers to Ireland. Although of Dalriadic stock, they came from Scotland in the thirteenth century and took over large areas in the North East. A small and separate branch of that family settled in Co. Clare where they too are still to be found.

CONCLUSION.

John de Courcy Ireland, Ireland's leading maritime historian, wrote on norman ships, what can only be a particularly apt summary of Ireland's seafaring background:

"The mesolithic, the neolithic, the bronze age, the Celtic-speaking, the Norse and the Norman-Gallo-Flemish Irish who came in successive waves to our shores all came of course, by sea, and between them, built a maritime tradition in this island second to none in the world".

GLOSSARY.

Adze	- a heavy chisel-like tool fastened at right angles to its wooden handle.
Bow	- the forward part of a vessel.
Carvel built	- built with the planks flush and not overlapping.
To caulk	- to fill or close a seam, make watertight.
Clinker built	- built with the planks overlapping downwards.
Coracle	- an almost round boat made like a wicker basket and then covered by hides or canvas.
Crannóg	- an ancient man-made lake dwelling, an artificial island.
Curragh	- a skin (nowadays tarred canvas) covered boat.
Gunwale	- the uppermost edge or rim of a vessel.
Latteen	- a triangular sail extended by a long, tapering yard.
Lee	- the side sheltered or turned away from the wind.
Mizzenmast	- the aftermost mast of a three masted vessel.
Portside	- the left side of a vessel when facing the bow.
Starboard	- the right side of a vessel when facing the bow.
Stern	- the afterend of a ship.
Strake	- a continuous line of planking on the side or bottom of a vessel.
Stringer	- a cross plank to keep horizontal timbers in position.
Strut	- a bar or timber to brace or support pressure in the direction of its length.
Thwart	- a seat across a boat, one used by an oarsman.
Withy	- a flexible twig.
Yardarm	- either end of a square rigged vessel's yard.

BIBLIOGRAPHY.

ANON:
  "Everyman's Encyclopedia" 1932.
BASS, George F.;
  "A History of Seafaring" 1972.
BASS, George F.;
  "Archaeology under Water" 1966.
BREFFNY, Brian de;
  "Irish Family Names" 1982.
BRONSTED, J.;
  "The Vikings" 1960.
CAMBRENSIS, Giraldus;
  "The History and Topography of Ireland"
  [Topographia Hiberniae] c. 1200.
CASSON, L.;
  "Sewn Boats" 1963.
CHARLESWORTH, J.K.;
  "The Geology of Ireland" 1953.
CLARKE, Hewson;
  "History of England" 1813.
COURCY IRELAND, John de;
  "Norman Ships" 1985.
COURCY IRELAND, John de;
  "Ireland and the Irish in Maritime History" 1986.
CRUMLIN-PEDERSEN, Ole;
  "From Viking Ships to Hanseatic Cogs" 1983.
CUNLIFFE, Barry;
  "The Celtic World".
CUSACK, M.F.;
  "A History of the Irish Nation" 1876.
EDWARDS, Ruth Dudley;
  "An Atlas of Irish History" 1973.

ELLMERS, Detlev;
  "Fruehmittelalterliche Handelsschiffahrt in Mittel-und Nordeuropa"
  1972.
ELLMERS, Detlev;
  "Keltischer Schiffbau".
ENGLEHARD, Conrad;
  "Denmark in the Early Iron Age" 1866.
EVANS, Estyn;
  "Irish Folkways" 1957.
FALLON, Niall;
  "The Armada in Ireland" 1978.
FARRELL, A.W.; PEENY, S.;
  "The Broighter Boat; A Reassessment" 1975.
FITZGERALD, Walter;
  "The Historical Geography of Early Ireland" 1925.
FOOTE, P. and WILSON, D.M.;
  "The Viking Achievement" 1970.
GREENHILL, Basil;
  "Archaeology of the Boat" 1976.
HALIDAY, Charles;
  "The Scandinavian Kingdom of Dublin" 1881.
HARDY, Evelyn;
  "Survivors of the Armada" 1966.
HARBISON, Peter;
  "The Archaeology of Ireland" 1976.
HARDEN, Donald;
  "The Phoenicians" 1962.
HARDIMAN, James;
  "The History of the Town and County of the Town of Galway"
  1820.
HARTMANN, A.;
  "Praehistorische Goldfunde aus Europa" 1970.
HORNELL, J.;
  "British Coracles and Irish Curraghs" 1938.

HORNELL, J.;
  "Water Transport" 1970.
JOHNSTONE, P.;
  "A Medieval Skin Boat" 1962.
JOHNSTONE, P.;
  "The Bantry Boat" 1964.
JOHNSTONE, P.;
  "Seacraft of Prehistory" 1980.
JONES, Gwyn;
  "A History of the Vikings" 1968.
JOYCE, P.W.;
  "A Social History of Ancient Ireland" 1903.
KNOX, H.T.;
  "The History of the County of Mayo" 1908.
LANDSTROM, Bjorn;
  "The Ship" 1961.
LETHBRIDGE, T.C.;
  "Boats and Boatmen" 1952.
LEWIS, Samuel;
  "A Topographical Dictionary of Ireland " 1837.
LONGFIELD, A.K.;
  "Anglo Irish Trade in the 16th Century" 1929.
MARMION, A.;
  "Maritime Ports of Ireland" 1856.
MASON, T.H.;
  "The Islands of Ireland" 1936.
MATTINGLY, Garrett;
  "The Armada" 1957.
MOLL, F.;
  "Das Schiff in der bildenden Kunst" 1929.
MOORE, Thomas;
  "The History of Ireland".
MOSCATI, Sabatino;
  "The World of the Phoenicians" 1968.

MAC ALISATER, R.A.S.;
"*The Archaeology of Ireland*" 1949.
MAC DONALD, Malcolm Ross;
"*The Search Begins*".
MC CALMONT, Rose E.;
"*Memoirs of the Binghams*" 1915.
MC GOWAN, Alan;
"*The Ship - Tiller and Whipstaff*" 1981.
MC GRAIL, Sean;
"*Logboats of England and Wales*" 1978.
MC GRAIL, Sean;
"*The Ship - Rafts, Boats and Ships*" 1981.
MAC MANUS, Seamas;
"*The Story of the Irish Race*" 1944.
MAC NEILL, Eoin;
"*Phases of Irish History*" 1968.
O'BRIEN, Maire and Conor Cruise;
"*A Concise History of Ireland*" 1972.
O'FLAHERTY, Roderic;
"*A Chorographical Description of West or H-Iar Connaught*"
1684 and 1846.
PIGGOTT, Stuart;
"*Ancient Europe*" 1965.
PLINY,
"*Naturalis Historia*" [transl. by H. Rackham 1942].
SEVERIN, Tim;
"*The Brendan Voyage*" 1978.
SOLINUS, Gaius Julius;
"*Collectanea Rerum Memorabilium or Polylistor*"
Book No. XXIII "Britannia" c. 300.
TACITUS, Publius or Gaius;
"*Histories*" [transl. by W.H. Fyfe 1908].
TORR, Cecil;
"*Ancient Ships*" 1895.

WAKEMAN, W.F.;
   "A Handbook of Irish Antiquities; Pagan and Christian" 1891.
WARE, Sir James;
   "The Antiquities and History of Ireland" 1705.
WOOD-MARTIN, W.G.;
   "The Lake Dwellings of Ireland" 1886.
WRIGHT, E.V.;
   "The North Ferriby Boats" a guide book 1976.

Other Publications by Ballinakella Press include

Houses of Clare, Hugh Weir
These My Friends & Forebears:
   The O'Briens at Dromoland, Grania R. O'Brien
Máire Rua: *Lady of Leamaneh,* Máire MacNeill
Murrough the Burner: *Murchadh na dTóiteán,* Ivar O'Brien
O'Dea: *The Story of a Rebel Clan,* Risteárd Ua Cróinín
Ireland - *A Thousand Kings,* edited Hugh Weir
Upper Lough Erne, Rev. William Henry (facsimile)
Ireland: *Sketches of Some Southern Counties,* G. Holmes (facsimile)
O'Brien: *People and Places,* Hugh Weir
O'Malley: *People and Places,* Sheila Mulloy (co-publication)
Burke: *People and Places,* Eamonn de Burca (co-publication)
Mac Carthy: *People and Places,* Alicia St Leger
O'Neill: *People and Places,* Sean O'Neill

Forthcoming Ballinakella Press Books

Houses of Kerry, Valerie Bary
The Encumbered Estates, Dr. Mary Lyons